Mystery Bay Monster

Margaret Fetty
Illustrated by Sean O'Neill

Rigby®
A Harcourt Achieve Imprint

www.Rigby.com
1-800-531-5015

"Vince, I got one!" said Keisha.

Vince went over to his sister and looked
at the little fish swimming in the net.

"You caught a spottail shiner," Vince said.
"They are silver and have a black dot
near their tails."

Vince drew the fish in his pad.

"You've drawn everything
we've seen on our vacation,"
said Keisha, letting the fish go.

Vince grinned and said, "I want
to draw everything I see here.
It will help me remember
all the great things we've done."

Just then Vince pointed out at the water.
"Look! Now I'm going to draw that!" he said.

Keisha looked up and saw something big and gray
swimming in the water.
It had a round head and flippers.
In a flash, it was gone.

"What was that?" Keisha asked.

"I don't know," said Vince as he finished
his drawing.
"I saw a library a few blocks away.
We can search for the answer there!"

Vince and Keisha looked at the drawing
as they walked with their mother
to the library.

"This picture reminds me of Nessie,
the famous Loch Ness monster,"
Vince said.

"I've heard of Nessie," said Keisha,
"but many people believe it's only a legend."

"Here," Vince said, drawing a quick picture.
"This is what Nessie looks like."

"Do you think we saw a monster?"
Keisha asked as they went
into the library.
"It was definitely real!"

"Monsters aren't real, though," said Mom.

The children picked out several books
about sea life and sat at a table.

"Maybe we saw a cownose ray," said Vince,
pointing to a photograph.
"It has a bump on its head,
and it has flippers."

Keisha studied the picture.
"The animal we saw didn't have a thin tail.
Its body was much longer, too," she said.

Keisha began looking through a book
about animals that live in the Chesapeake Bay.
She stopped at a photograph
of an animal that looked like a snake.

"There is a legend about a monster living
in Chesapeake Bay!" Keisha said excitedly.
"Its name is Chessie."

Vince held his drawing next to the photograph.
"The head looks the same," he said.
"The book says that Chessie has flippers, too."

Keisha said sadly, "But the animal we saw had
a round body instead of a snake's body.
I don't think we saw Chessie.
I guess it's just a legend after all."

"Hey, look at this!" said Vince.
"There's an animal that swims in the bay.
Many people think it's Chessie, the bay monster.
But it's really a manatee.
Most people call it Chessie."

Keisha looked at the picture of the manatee.
"The head and the flippers look the same," she said.

"The length and size are about right," said Vince.

"I think we found our bay monster!" Mom said.

"I still have some paper," said Vince.
"Let's go find Chessie."

"Which Chessie?" Keisha asked.

"I would love to see Chessie the bay monster," said Vince, "but I think we will be seeing Chessie the mystery manatee!"